Clean Your Room!

A Girl's Guide To Mental Organization

Clean Your Room!
A Girl's Guide To Mental Organization

ISBN: 978-0692382981
Copyright ©2014, Zion Signature Investments, LLC
All rights reserved

Printed in the United States of America by CreateSpace

Table of Content

Preface

1. Go Back to Get Back

2. Forgiveness

3. Goals

4. Do Your Inventory

5. Let It Go

6. "Self" Talk

7. Attitude

8. Confidence

9. Strength

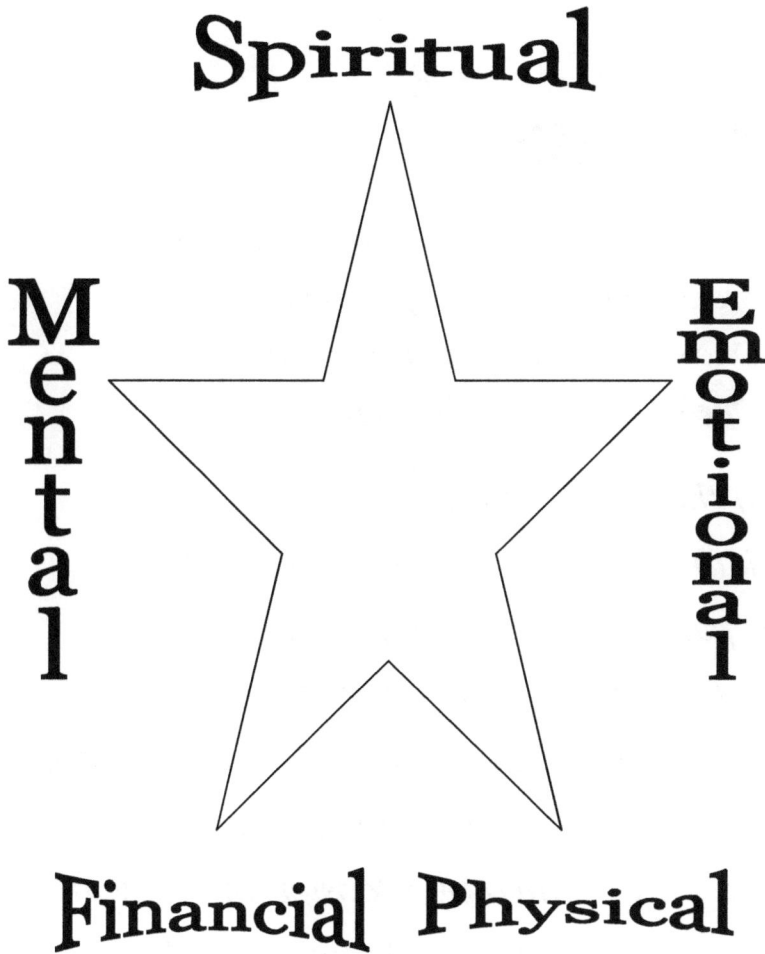

Preface

self (self) N. – 1. The identity, character, or essential qualities of any person or thing. 2. One's own person as distinct from all others. 3. One's own welfare of interest.

In the above definition, "self" is a noun defined by other nouns that all have separate meanings of their own. Those definitions come together to provide the meaning for one word that describes you. Your identity, character, and qualities are not only defined by Webster, but they are also defined by you. Your internal definition of you is far more important than what society says is normal. Your identity is your individuality which is enhanced by your charter, or behavior which produces special qualities within you. In this book, you will probably see some similarities between you and the author. Life's many challenges are often times very difficult. However, if we learn to embrace them, then our challenges can bring opportunities for growth.

Clean Your Room!

A Girl's Guide To Mental Organization

While watching TV one day, I channel surfed to the Dr. Phil show. Now, I normally don't care to watch Dr. Phil or any other talk show for that matter, but I decided to see what he had to say. Featured on the show that day was a man that was a compulsive liar. This man lied so much to his family that he didn't realize that he was lying when didn't have to lie. What bothered me about the situation was that this was a full grown adult that found every excuse that he could to not own up to his problem. It seemed in the beginning that he thought it was okay, but I thought he was a jerk for it. He just would not see himself as a liar. He thought he was just doing what he had to do. Then, all of a

11

sudden, but simultaneously, Dr. Phil and I said these words, "You can't change what you don't acknowledge." I was floored. I could not believe it. I try hard not to agree with Dr. Phil. I am not sure why. It may be that I believe that Dr. Phil has been branded as "the great and powerful Oz" of psychology. He is the biggest know–it–all and is in everybody's business. Yet, here I am agreeing with him. Although I try very hard to disagree with Dr. Phil, it never happens. We always agree. I just chalk it up to great minds thinking alike.

In saying the words, "you can't change what you don't acknowledge," in judgment of the couple on the show, I saw something about my "self" that I needed to work on.

God showed me His since of humor that day. By using someone that I thought was a know-it-all, fully opinionated, in your business big mouth, God showed me what I needed to do to improve who I was. I was able to acknowledge my own issues, and began to see them as challenges that were opportunities for growth. Since then, I have continued to see all challenges as a chance to enhance my "self". So, thank you Dr. Phil.

Growth gives way to grace. I had to look at my own growth or lack thereof, to understand why my "self" was at what seemed like its lowest point. Some of you may be at this point with your "self". You may not have an understanding about your "self", and how you are in control of it. You are in control of your identity. You are in control of your character. You are in control of your qualities. You are in control of your emotions. You are in control of your "self".

"…let faith be the bridge you build to overcome evil and welcome good."

-Dr. Maya Angelou

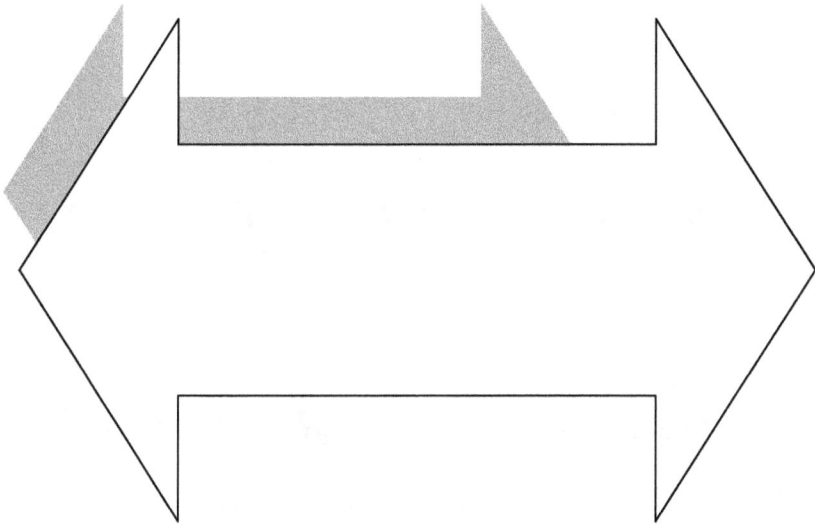

1

Go Back to Get Back

Revisit Your Past to Regain Your Future

In the beginning, a beautiful baby was presented to the world. Her proud parents unaware of the real task that they faced as this new little life looked at them with trusting eyes. Well…we all want to make it perfect for our children, but because we ourselves are not perfect things do not always turn out the way we thought they

18

would at first glance. Many of our patterns and processes come from things gleaned from when we were first presented to the world. Our developing minds were then, and still are like sponges soaking up every ounce of everything spilled before us. We were filled with things that have stayed with us to this day. Our minds came on the scene as empty rooms in our temples. Now, our rooms have become filled with so much clutter that our temples are experiencing growing pains. Spiritual, mental, emotional, physical, and financial pains that all may stem from the overload of bad information that we have been carrying around since birth, in addition to all of the bad information that we have collected up to this point. It is time for us to clean our

19

rooms. The room…is our mind. It is time for us to get our rooms organized in order to have clarity about those things that we need to discover our full potential, and move forward with confidence into our given destiny. The light of our star will burn much brighter lighting our path to prosperity. Here is where I started.

I often watched and listened helplessly as my father abused my mother. He would yell at her saying horrible things, push her around, and hit her. I hated that fact that he did that. I remember my sisters and me sitting at the foot of the bed watching TV one morning while my parents fought. I was about four or five years old at the time and I really don't remember what the fight was about. I just wanted it to be over. I turned around just in time to see my mother bleeding from her mouth. I wanted to protect her from the monster that my father had become. He definitely was not my daddy that day.

I guess he noticed the damage that he had done and left the room. That was my chance to get closer to my mother. I ran over to the side of the bed where her head was in hopes that it would make her feel better. Instead it helped to ruin my perception of what I believed my father was to us. I thought we were the typical happy family, but that image was quickly destroyed by the swelling of my mother's lip, and the blood on the sheet. My father runs back into the bedroom with a dirty towel and the cold water bottle from the refrigerator. The look in his eyes was not of urgency, but anger. He began yelling at me for standing next to my mother not concerned about either one of our feelings nor did he care about my attempt to comfort her. I was so scared. It felt like he was angry with me for seeing what he had done to my mother. He made me feel like it was my fault when he shouted, "Now go sit down." I began to cry. As I turned to walk away from my mother's side of the bed back over to where my sisters sat perfectly still watching Sesame Street, my mother grabbed my arm and pulled me back over to where she was. I knew then that I was supposed to protect my mother. At least that was what I thought at the time, but being as young as I was I didn't realize that being in the middle of my parents was not the best place for me. I believe that in that moment is where I picked up a willingness to protect those close to me without regard for my own "self." There was no way I was going to leave my mother for a second time. Subconsciously, suppressing my feelings and only considering those of others stuck with me.

As a child, I would take on the problems of others, and defend them in my mind. In my imagination I could say what I wanted to protect someone else, but continued to hold in my own problems. All I needed was a mirror and my own reflection to speak at and to regarding the treatment of others. Now, I am not saying that I had the worst upbringing in the world, but I must admit that it was close. A little girl's harsh start made way for much heartache as I continued to grow into adulthood.

My father seemed to just fade out of my life after that. I don't remember seeing him at all after that day. He went missing and so did my typical happy family. Normal for us was no hugs, no kisses, no I love you, no family time, no mother daughter time, no, no, no, and no. If I were to venture a guess as to why there was never any affection between us, I would say it was simply because there was none in generations up to that point. If it was not experienced by our elders, then our elders could not teach it to us. I believe that we were just expected to know that the person that did for you, loved you. Love was an assumption, never taught or expressed verbally. My father was not much the affectionate type, and unfortunately neither was my mother.

I didn't know what a good touch was. So, I could not tell you what a bad touch felt like. How could I? I had no direction. I learned from what I saw. Guidance? Well…that was the lady in the elementary school office that put together all of our school plays. We called her our guidance counselor. She did a pretty good job counseling us on how we needed to remember our lines for performances, to be quiet in the cafeteria while the other children were rehearsing, and that "reading is fundamental." I remember playing the role of an angel in the kindergarten play. Yet I don't ever remember feeling angelic at all. I always felt like everything was not quite right. I was never at peace with anything, and always very unsure about making decisions, and uneasy with my surroundings. Unfortunately, I carried these emotions and feelings throughout elementary school, junior and senior high school, and right into adulthood.

My mother had done the best that she could with us. After my father decided to finally leave us, my mother raised me and my three siblings by herself. She worked very hard to finish school, get a job, and later purchased a home for us outside of the project complex that we had to move into. Thankfully, my grandparents helped, and my aunt and uncle did all they could to make sure that my mother did not feel that she had to do it all alone. Still, the junk found a place in my room to sit and wait for optimal moments to cloud my future judgments.

Later in my adult life I was diagnosed with a mental disorder. I discovered through months of therapy that my issues came from feelings about situations that have been suppressed in my subconscious mind. The voices that I heard were those hidden feelings, and emotions trying to make sure that I knew that they were there. Those visions that I continuously saw made sure that I did not forget those feelings that I had suppressed years ago. Deep down underneath all of the years of clutter was the very reason why I could not make productive choices. I could not bring my "self" to see a positive future, because (subconsciously) of my negative past.

If my mind was a representation of a bedroom, then my bedroom was junky. I could not get to the things I needed all because of the clutter in my room. The poor choices, mixed emotions, misplaced anger were all representations of clutter in my mind that I had been accumulating from those early days of my childhood. I came to the realization that my future, and the future of my children depended on the cleanliness of my room, or lack thereof. I had to begin the process of removing the clutter. Layers of junk had to be removed, surfaces had to be wiped down, fresh paint had to be applied, and new furniture and accessories brought in. I saw my "self" in a new and brighter light…and so will you.

As you begin the journey to clean up your room, you may have to turn on some light in order to see what lies in those dark corners. The reason why those things are buried in those dark corners is simply because they were put there many years ago and you never went back to address them. Then, we continued to pile other things on top of them, our issues and issues of others as well, all the while those things buried in the dark corners of our minds continued to fester and take on a silent life of their own deep within the shadows of our minds. As children we are not always equipped to handle certain situations in order to keep our minds clear. In some cases we are taught to keep quiet, or never allowed to express ourselves. Instead of letting it out, we hold those issues, ills, pains, and feelings of contempt in our minds having never received validation for our feelings which creates the start of a junky room.

Subconsciously, we are cultivating unwritten laws planted by negative states that we allow to govern the way we behave. Why is that? Let's take a look a the way the subconscious and conscious mind work against each other and some of the things we can do to reverse the current subconscious dominance that is keeping our room full of useless clutter.

Conscious   Subconscious   Unconscious

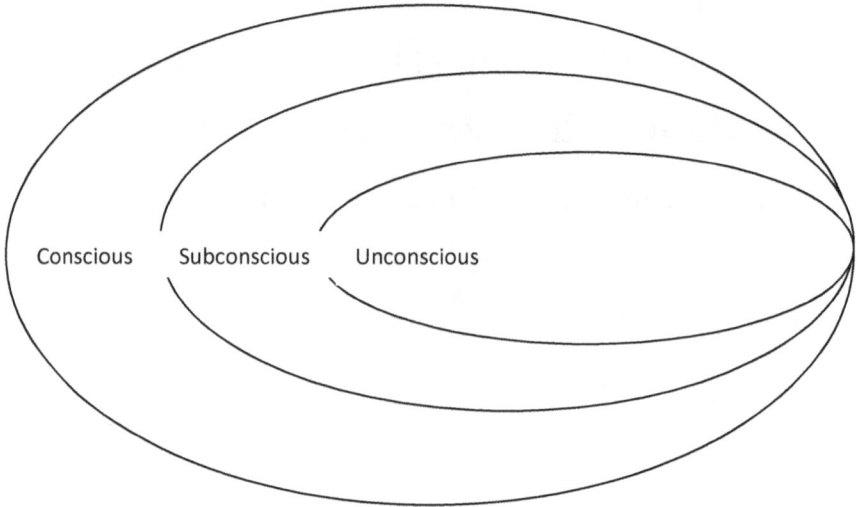

Our room (or mind), has three levels the conscious, subconscious, and the unconscious. The unconscious mind is where we automatically process actions. Body functions are things that we do without any thought at all. For instance, we do not have to tell our heart to beat, or lungs to breath. Unconsciously, it happens (Thank God!). However, our conscious mind is where we process new data. Intellectually, we analyze and make immediate decisions within our conscious mind. The subconscious mind or the dark corners of our room, is where we store all of our long term memory. Those childhood experiences that have stayed with us this whole time have been stored in our subconscious mind. All of our feelings and emotions also come from our subconscious mind. Our subconscious mind takes up most of our brain and is more powerful than the conscious mind. This is why I believe the subconscious mind is constantly taking over when we attempt to respond to the calls of our destiny.

Seeds of defeat were planted in our subconscious mind from birth. Any negative experience that we had was planted in our subconscious mind and stamped as law. Most laws are created to protect us, but in essence certain laws have a negative effect on us. Once we understand that we have the power to change those negative paradigms, then and only then can we take the necessary actions to create our own laws. Although we can lean on previous experiences to help structure our laws, we must be very careful to not allow those same experiences to in fact hinder our new laws.

Look at it this way. You are your own country. Your house/temple is your body.

It is where you live in your country, and you are the commander-in-chief. The President of the United States of

_____ (insert your name here). Your brain is the owner's suite in your home, or the Oval Office. Your mind is where all the decisions are made, and as the boss or leader of your own free world, you must make decisions that benefit all involved. Making decisions based solely on emotions could prove to be detrimental. It is obvious that you cannot allow feelings and emotions lead by the negative processes of the subconscious mind run your country. It is best made with the conscious minds intellectual process with careful consideration of the subconscious mind.

You may have had a painful childhood experience that has become subconsciously the law for all of your decisions regarding any subject. Look back at your star (Diagram 1). What decisions have you made based on a subconscious law? Maybe you have chosen a certain religion based on what you were raised with. It is also possible that you have trouble with financial freedom because of a subconscious law regarding money. If you were abused as a child, then it is quite possible that you have a subconscious law that states that you cannot trust anyone because of that emotional or physical scaring left by someone else's actions. You may not have been encouraged to express your thoughts so that you feel mentally stagnant. I have been here, even today in my adult life. I have found the five points on my star to be dull on several occasions, but I have discovered that I am in control of the brightness of my own star. I can change the laws in my United States, and I can change the bulbs in my star…and so can you.

I believe you are ready to create a new set of laws. I believe that you are ready to change the bulbs in your star. You are ready to take action. The fact that you are reading this book shows your impeccable strength and willingness to clean your room. Up until now it has been an overwhelming task. However, it is now time to make your first conscious decision

to do what is best, and what will benefit
your temple, and strengthen you while you
become the number one superpower. Get
your brooms and dust pans, and strap on
your aprons because it is high time you
CLEAN YOUR ROOM!

"Hate, it has caused a lot of problems in the world, but has not solved one yet."

-Dr. Maya Angelou

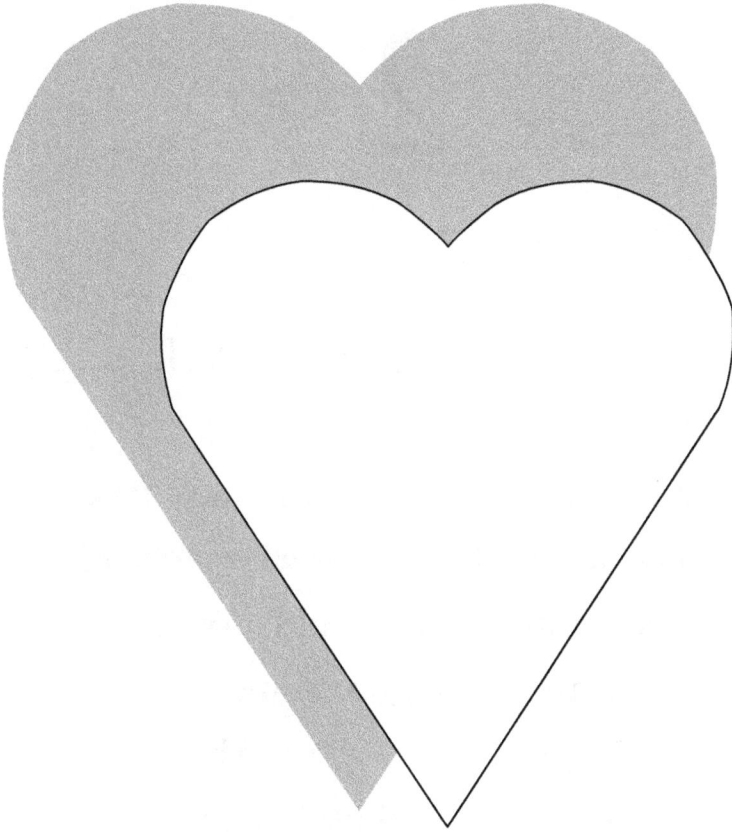

2

Forgiveness

Don't Just Get It, Give It

We hold on to our past in most cases mainly because it has become comfortable, or we need some kind of validation, or because we are looking for some sort of closure. However, if we were to be totally honest with ourselves, those are just excuses for us to hold on to past pains. These excuses are what support the subconscious laws that have become extra junk in our rooms. This worthless negative

42

junk that we really do not need in order to reach our full potential often blocks our ability to even see a positive future for ourselves. It is within our power to make a choice to remove these excuses that we have allowed to grow in to powerful pieces of clutter in the dark corners of our rooms.

How do we start to remove this clutter? Make a decision today to forgive that someone or something that may have caused you harm in the past. State boldly to that person, or situation that they will no longer have control over your room. If you allow that past pain to create laws, then you are not the boss. You are not the President of YOUR United States of

_____. That power that

belongs to you is given to the other person or to that situation. In forgiveness, we take our power back.

Same thing holds true with fear. Fear is another learned law that keeps us bound mentally. It is a law created by an experience that was never dispelled. The law of fear keeps us from taking the step that starts our journey of 1,000 miles to fulfillment, 1,000 miles to our promise, 1,000 miles to our destiny, 1,000 miles to our place of peace. We hide behind the fear factor to the point where we cannot see beyond it. What if just on the other side of that fear was God's true promise for you? The battle with fear is a constant struggle for some, but let me encourage you that somewhere in your "room" is a sling shot called decision. Pick it up and load it with a rock called faith. Take aim at your giant called fear; pull back on the band called courage, and fire your faith right between the eyes of fear. It's not just in fairy tales that giants get slayed, and if that is what you believe, then its time you wrote your own story about how you made a decision, and took action that lead you to your own prosperity.

Honesty is another law that we believe has many technicalities. Some believe that a little lie is better than hurting someone's feelings, or calling someone out, or disappointing someone. Well...this is not always the case. Surely you have heard that if you tell one lie, you will eventually have to tell another lie to cover that first untruth...and then another lie, and another. Maybe even another lie. This will only increase the junk in your room. Why? Simply because you have to keep the first lie in your mind as to not forget what you said in order to keep the lie alive and well with the person that you lied to for whatever reason you chose to lie in the first place. Clear as mud, huh? This is another reason to just simply tell the truth.

Some of us even have the audacity to lie to our own selves as if we don't know the truth. We lie about our feelings in order to accommodate the feelings of others. We lie to make ourselves look better, or to gain respect. We constantly play roles lying and pretending to be something that we are not so much so that we began to believe our own lie which continuously adds junk in our room. Before we know it, we are consumed with all of the junk that we have allowed to build up in our room and we cannot keep up. This builds anxiety, which causes stress, which can lead to problems with health and relationships with others as well as our selves.

Now is the time to forgive the decision to forego honesty. No more hoarding lies. Those days are gone and you are now in a new undertaking to ensure that your room is no longer full of the clutter of lies that you thought you needed to tell in order to prove something, or spare someone else's feelings. Today you can accept that there is no other option except to tell the truth. This may seem hard at first, but you will find that over time it becomes much easier and those who see you as a straight shooter will respect you even more.

Some clutter is only removable by the act of simple forgiveness, but other forms of clutter take specific forgiveness. If your best girlfriend borrows $50, and never pays you back, then this is simple forgiveness because you understand that you should never loan what you cannot afford to give away. On the other hand, serious wounds that ultimately put you in a victim scenario may take a much stronger decision. Abuse comes in many forms and takes a toll on our rooms the longer we allow it to fester in the dark corners. This kind of clutter actually carries a bad aroma that is easily detected by anyone that wants to take advantage of you. Let's call them gnats. You have seen how spoiled apples attract gnats, and this is the best way to describe what is happening to spoiled emotions. The saying, "one bad apple spoils the bunch." Well, that is definitely the case here, as one bad emotion spoils the entire room.

Try thinking of forgiveness as a big bucket of bleach. Everyone knows that tough cleaning jobs require tough cleaning products. Bleach is my go-to cleaning agent. Depending on the cleaning job, I will add a little bleach to my bucket, or a lot. You must consider your own cleaning job and if you need help lifting your bucket of forgiveness. Many doctors, life coaches, and even pastors are available to help you with your cleansing. If you discover that your cleaning job may become a bit overwhelming, then I would encourage you to seek a professional to help you get the job done.

Seeking wise counsel is what I am suggesting. Not that of someone that enables you to hold on to clutter. You know who they are…that so-called best friend that "always has your back," will co-sign your pity party paperwork as soon as you hand them the pen. If your BFF has a junky room as well, then this may not be the one to help you. Now I hate to say this, but if both of you have junky rooms then the most you will do for each other is compete to see which one of you has the most clutter, possibly swap clutter, and then come away with the same amount of clutter if not more. You must keep your need to de-clutter your room free from any extra clutter. Sometimes a great friend can have the best intentions, but the worst advice and that is the last thing you need.

Always consider the source. If the person that you are considering confiding in has a junky room themselves, then maybe you should seek other counsel. I would never say that person can't help because no matter where anyone is in life, there is some kind of lesson that could be gleaned from their experience, but does it make sense to ask a person that doesn't have a million dollars…how to make a million dollars? Hmmm…let that one marinate.

"I believe the most important single thing beyond discipline and creativity, is daring to dare."

-Dr. Maya Angelou

3

Goals

Dream much?

Is there something that you really want? What is that one thing that you cannot stop thinking about? Whether it is a great career, a wonderful relationship, happy and healthy children, millions of dollars in the bank, or just to be satisfied with life there must be something that drives you. What are you passionate about? What are your dreams?

Clean Your Room!

A Girl's Guide To Mental Organization

Some of us can't grasp a hold of our dreams because of all of the extra stuff in our room. There is no place for dreams to survive amongst clutter and confusion. Throw in a dream and your room may become overwhelmed. Your room may even become frustrated because you can't see a way to achieve your dreams because of all of the clutter that is blocking the view of your vision. It is time to give your dreams a pathway to progress.

Now here is the tricky part. You must make a decision which requires action. Have you ever tried to sweep a floor by just simply thinking about it? What about packing boxes, or wiping off a table? You cannot do it without some movement on your part. You must take some kind of action. The decision making process is not as complicated as one may think. First, you must identify the decision that you must make. Second, explore your options. Third, gather as much information as you need to make your decision. The next thing that you must do is make your decision and TAKE ACTION. Now you must also take into consideration the consequences of your action and determine if they are good or bad. Of course we always want to reap good consequences, but the risk factor could be a bit higher and could take our action to a different result than we had originally planned. Therefore, we must remember to take action with a proper "Plan B", the backup plan.

Let's lay this out so that it is easy for you to understand, and so that you can see your own decision making process unfold. We will use our title for the following decision scenario. You will see how simple it is to follow along, and in no time you will write your own outline with confidence.

Five Step Decision Making Process

Step 1

Identify the decision

Clean my room. I must remove all of
the things in my room that I do not
need and clear the space from all of
the clutter

Step 2

Identify your options

Leave it junky

Call someone to do it for me

Ignore the clutter

Just get started

Step 3

Gathering information

A clean and organized room is much safer for me to operate in, and increases my ability to move freely throughout my space

A clean room is also a picture of how I run my country. A clean room just looks better than a junky room

Step 4

Make the decision and take action

I am going to clean my room today. I will create a box marked "Items to throw away" and a box marked

"Items to keep" and place them .
outside of the room yet close .
enough to walk over and drop .
things into as I begin cleaning .

Step 5

Evaluation

This was the appropriate decision .
because my room is clean and .
clear of clutter and I am able to see
the room and uncover lost treasures
that were buried underneath all of
the mess...namely the real me .

Yes…that's right. The real you is hiding under all of that clutter and messiness that is has piled up in your room. The decision making process will help you clean your room and free your mind from all of the things that have taken over your ability to make sound judgments. A better you is waiting. The you that is in your dreams is waiting for an opportunity to soar out from under your junky room. Copy the blank decision making outline and determine what decision you must make. More importantly, follow through with your decision and then let's get to work on some of those dreams that have been on hold for way too long.

It's your turn. Follow the decision making process on the next few pages. Write down every thought that comes to mind regarding a decision that you have been struggling to make, and don't concern your "self" with right or wrong answers. Just write down your thoughts, then go back to review your process.

Five Step Decision Making Process

Step 1

Identify the decision

_____

_____

_____

_____

_____

_____

_____

_____

_____

_____

_____

_____

_____

Step 2

Identify your options

_____

_____

_____

_____

_____

_____

_____

_____

_____

_____

_____

_____

_____

_____

Step 3

Gathering information

_____

_____

_____

_____

_____

_____

_____

_____

_____

_____

_____

_____

_____

_____

Step 4

Make the decision and take action

_____

_____

_____

_____

_____

_____

_____

_____

_____

_____

_____

_____

_____

_____

Step 5

Evaluation

_____

_____

_____

_____

_____

_____

_____

_____

_____

_____

_____

_____

_____

Congratulations on your decision. Now that you have made your decision, let's move forward with those dreams. You have had a dream in your heart, and a vision of what your life could be. It had been stashed there from childhood and then, life happened. But now, we have a nice clean room to start with and that dream has the ability to become a reality. As you have seen in the previous exercise, all it takes is a decision and then action. Your accomplishment is within reach, and clear defined goals will help you get there.

Anyone can say they have a goal to be rich. "I want to have a lot of money," but the problem with this statement is that it is only a statement. It lacks definition, clarity, and if you are only saying this without a plan, then it's just words. We need to get those words on paper and turn them in to an achievable goal with a clear path to success. Believe it or not, we can schedule our success. And along with much prayer, good decisions, and the power of action we can accomplish our goals and achieve success.

Remember that things must be done decent and in order, but they also should be done SMART. Working smarter and not harder will decrease tension and levels of frustrations when problems arise. Organize your goals using the **SMART** method. Goals should be:

Specific

Measurable

Attainable

Relevant

Time sensitive

I want to have a lot of money is not a **SMART** goal. It does not answer who, what, where, when, why, or how. It is important that you have all of these questions answered in order to have a well defined goal to start your planning and your decision making process. Consider this instead:

My personal short term goal is to improve my finances by consulting a financial planner for guidance in implementing a savings plan this month in which I will deposit $5,000 into my investment account by the 30th of each month in order to save $60,000 by December 31st.

Talk about **SMART**! This is just an example of a financial goal, but what about one for your newly clean room. Consider starting like this:

My long term goal is to keep my mental, and emotion state clear from clutter by enlisting the help of wise counsel, a mentor, or a life coach. I will schedule weekly meetings with my counselor and develop *strategies to continue making positive changes in my life by the 30th day of this month.*

Okay…this is an exaggeration of what you might consider, or what you need to keep you on track. However, if you aren't careful, then with every speed bump or difficult moment you will unconsciously start to pile clutter in your room again, and that's a no, no to the third degree. Moving forward after a long time habit of learning how to work while standing still is not an easy task, but with the proper resources you will learn to adopt the habit of constant forward motion regardless of how high the speed bump may be.

Take a moment to consider your own goals. What do you want to achieve within the next six months? Within the next year? And within the next five years? You want to make your goals stick to the SMART model and be sure to write them down and keep them in a place where you can see them often. This way you will begin to train your brain to focus on your goals and the new lessons that teach you to prioritize what is most important to you, and not the old lessons that have taught you that your dreams are not important.

"All great achievements require time."

-Dr. Maya Angelou

4

Do Your Inventory

What you do and do not need?

I remember participating in a team building exercise that required our team to complete a very strange task. I had never seen this before and was quite puzzled when we were handed our orders. While sitting in the conference room, the instructor handed four people in each group blind folds. Before putting on their blind folds, the instructor tells the group that we are to walk as a group out to the parking lot where there was a bucket strategically placed in the center of four construction cones. Just outside of the construction cones, there was another bucket with various tools inside of it. To complete the task, we had to move the bucket that was inside of the cones to the outside of the cones.

Sounds simple right? Well…not so much. We were further instructed that we had to use the tools provided, and that only the blind folded team members could touch the tools. The rules went one step further as we were not to walk inside of the circle and the exercise was timed. WHAT?! Well needless to say we failed miserably. There was so much confusion. Everyone had their own way of completing the task, and it was obvious that everyone wanted the group to use their own individual thought process. Chaos and confusion took over the parking lot as everyone began the attempt to steer the blinded team members to the bucket of tools, and back towards the bucket that we were charged to move. A few team members stood back and chattered amongst themselves while others were extremely vocal in their commands. The blinded team members were helpless as all of the team members spoke directions from all directions. It was a ball of confusion.

After we were allowed to stumble over our own selves for what seemed like an eternity, the instructor finally stopped the exercise and asked us this question, "Have you done an inventory analysis?" The words were so powerful that the sky parted and the glow of the sun cast a bright spot light on our intelligence that had been in the dark for the past 45 minutes.

We all went over to the bucket and took a look at all of the tools inside. There were several different objects including four ropes, and a tire inner tube. The other objects were irrelevant, but somehow we managed to focus on all of the irrelevant objects and not the tools that were given to us to complete the task.

Does this sound familiar? It is the same thing that happens within our mind.

When we attempt to complete a task, all of the irrelevant things get in the way. We must do our inventory. By deciding what we need to complete the task and what we do not need will help us to not waste any time by using the wrong tools. This is a part of the planning process which should follow the decision making process.

We have made a decision to clean our room. Now we must line up our task and complete our inventory analysis. Our tasks include:

- removing the clutter from the room
- making the bed
- washing the windows
- wiping of all flat surfaces
- sweeping the floors

What items do I already have in order to complete these tasks?

- Time
- Broom
- Dust pan
- Cleaning solution
- Wiping Cloth

What items do I need to get in order to complete each task?

- Trash bin
- Recycle bin
- Some help

In the previous chapter, you had an opportunity to think about your goals. Let's use one of your goals to do another exercise. This time you are going to use your own decision to clean your room to create task and complete an inventory analysis of your own. No need to over think this or make it complicated. You will simply jot down what comes to mind for each goal. For example:

Goal: To lose 20 pounds at the end of the next two months by measuring my weight every Monday of each week, exercising a minimum of two hours per day, six days per week, consuming only 2000 calories within a 24 hour period. (Clean Your Room)

Task:
- Get a method of tracking your progress (removing the clutter from the room)
- Incorporate your exercise plan into your daily schedule (making the bed)
- Plan you meals in advance (washing the windows)

- Remove all unhealthy foods from the house (sweeping the floors)

What items do I already have in order to complete each task?
- A good attitude (Time)
- Positive energy (Broom)
- Strength (Dust pan)
- Commitment (Wiping cloth)

What items do need to get in order to complete each task?
- Healthy food (Trash bin)
- Personal trainer/Nutritionist (Recycle bin)
- Mentor/Coach (Some help)

Now it's your turn. Follow the same outline for your inventory analysis. Remember, don't think too much. Take the first thing that comes to mind and jot it down. Simply walk into your room, pick up the first thing you see, and work with it.

Goal:

_____

_____

_____

_____

_____

_____

Task:

- _____
- _____
- _____
- _____

What items do I already have in order to complete each task?

- _____
- _____
- _____
- _____

What items do I need to get in order to complete each task?

- _____
- _____
- _____
- _____

You can use this outline for either business or personal goals. Just remember to use the SMART acronym to help keep your "self" on track to success. It's okay to make adjustments when necessary. You must reevaluate often to make sure you are hitting your benchmarks, and take the appropriate actions when you are not. Do not think of this as step back. Remember, it is okay to go back to revisit, but it is not okay to go back to stay.

"You may encounter many defeats, but you must not be defeated."

-Dr. Maya Angelou

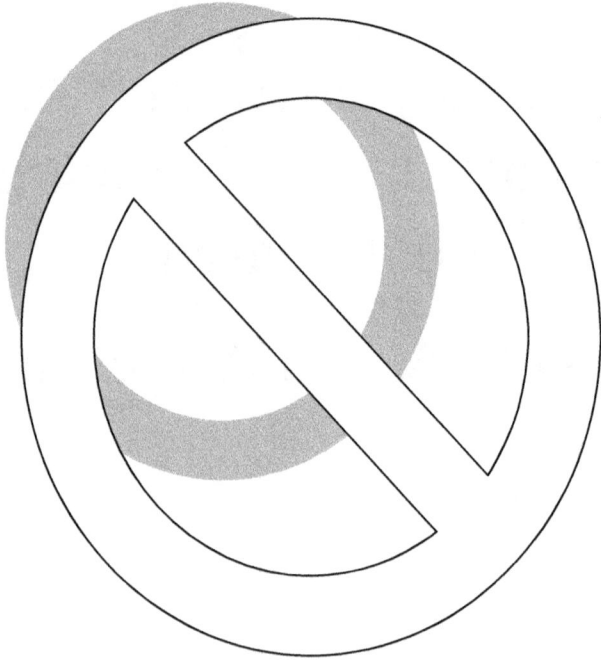

5

Let it go

Failure is not final.

I can remember a time back in my high school algebra class when I was given a test that consisted of only four questions worth 25 points apiece. Solve for y were the only directions, and the test took the entire hour to complete. My classmates and I did not believe that the test was fair simply because if you missed two questions...you failed. One question took an entire sheet of paper to solve for the answer. Most of us did not do well on this test. As the teacher was grading the test, she found that the mistake was made in the beginning of the problem. Something as simple as a misplaced symbol in the second line of the equation threw off the entire sequence and resulted in the wrong answer.

Life is very similar to this. It takes time to figure out the answer to life's problems, and the majority of the time when we get the wrong answer, it is simply a mistake in something we did in the beginning. This particular teacher was not so forgiving. Just like the universe, she allowed the grade to count. And also, just like the universe, she gave us an opportunity to redeem ourselves. "Practice makes perfect," she would say. For the next few lessons, we practiced, and we practiced. Our teacher assigned more and more of the problems on a weekly basis. We endured class work, home work, lunch time tutoring, after school tutoring, and peer training. She encouraged us to try harder, focus, and concentrate. Over 50% of my class failed the test, but after a few more weeks of studying more than 80% made passing grades...including me. It wasn't easy, but we got through it.

After failing that test, I began to find fault with every detail about it. I just knew that when I failed that test, it was totally not my fault. In my mind, I believed that I was set up to fail. I even went as far to say that the teacher simply did not like me. I told my grandfather who worked at the school that the teacher did not like me. I told him that she was on a power trip and wanted me to fail. Surely that sounds ridiculous now, but at the time I believed it. Something about that 'F' next to my name gave me reasons find every excuse in the world to concede to failure. Thankfully, with age comes wisdom.

Several people that we deem successful have seen a failure or two, or three, or 1,000 before they reached the level of success that they have accomplished. If those people had allowed themselves to succumb to the failures, then who knows where they would be right now. Anyone with a career in sales knows that it takes 10 no's before you get one yes. (Thank God!) We have to learn from failed experiences. In those failures are teachable moments that we can glean knowledge, understanding, and wisdom. If you fail ten times, then you really have just discovered 10 ways not to do it. Or in the case of the algebra test, I learned several ways to not solve for y. However, I learned that in solving for the answer, I was strengthening my room and adding much needed accessories that helped make my room more attractive.

As a real estate agent, I have seen many model homes. They are brand new, and staged perfectly. The furniture and accessories are all complimentary to the function of the room. The model home is strictly for show, and left untouched, the rooms are perfect. I have also seen homes that are lived in by a large family. They also have furniture and accessories that compliment the function of the room. However, these rooms are not for show, so they aren't always perfect. Maybe several times during the course of a day the rooms in the lived in home are cluttered or in disarray. Then, someone makes an effort to clean the room. The next day, the room may become cluttered again, and then someone makes an effort to clean the room once again. (Normally in my house…it's me.)

My point here is simple. Keeping a room clean in a lived in home takes work. You may have to clean the same room over, and over again, but each time you clean you enhance the room and keep the room's function clear. Being successful at anything takes work. And believe me…it's worth it.

"Success is liking yourself, liking what you do, and liking how you do it."

-Dr. Maya Angelou

6

"Self" Talk

Know what I'm saying…to my "self".

If I had a dime for every bad decision, or failure, then I would definitely be a millionaire. Truth is, many times we mentally quit before we even allow ourselves to try. We dare to dream big, and then when it comes time to take action we tend to allow what we did not do consume us. The negative voices in our room begin

103

to talk us out of making a decision that will lead towards action. Positive or negative, we can't move in either direction because of what we tell our own "self". So, our dream that we know will move us into the next level doesn't move any further than just a dream. It is halted by the stuff in our room. This is why we must address the hidden clutter.

I remember my first attempt at running a business. I was much younger and thought that I had a future in selling cosmetics. There was already a business plan in place and I need nothing more than to follow it. This internationally known company gave me the tools needed to be successful and surely I was up for becoming the best saleswomen they had ever seen. I have always been a take charge person so being my own boss was what I was born to do. So, what kept me from success in this business?

I have taken a few courses in business and few seminars locally and online. I decided after a few years in the military that I would come home and try to go back to school. I wanted to earn an MBA and JD degree. I thought I needed this piece of paper in order to not only be successful, but in order to be taken seriously. So, I talked my "self" out of completing the top sales goal because of what I told my "self"...I needed to do something else in order to be successful at my current task. I told my "self" that I could not be successful because I was not validated by a piece of paper. However, after taking inventory of what was underneath the clutter of my room, I found that the validation that I was seeking was not from the degree.

I have had several different business ideas over the years. Unfortunately, none of them have gone very far. I had a few clients here and there, but never enough to retire on. I remember my online clothing store. I sold women's suits and shoes online. I thought that because I admired the more mature women that wore big hats and beautiful suits to church that I could make a buck on designing, and selling those hats, suits, and accessories online. I also have a little obsession with beautiful shoes, so with the help of a mentor I wrote a business plan for a retail store. This was the perfect business for me, or so I thought.

One day after a bad comment from someone that was not relevant, I began to tell my "self" that the reason that I was unsuccessful in this business was because I knew nothing about business and I needed a business degree in order to make this business work. Again, validation by the piece of paper, or what it something else?

Over the years, I have been told on several occasions that I have "missed my calling." Now I still to this day don't know what my "calling" is, but I do know that I want as much as God's will is for my life and the life of my children. I have been chasing my own dreams for years and in chasing those dreams, I have discovered the possible reasons as to why I have not been as successful as I set out to be much sooner. I always start out well, and with good intentions. However, my "self" talk would not agree with my well placed intentions. I still felt like I was incomplete in business because of the lack of documented education.

I owned a small online boutique, as well as a life coaching and speaking business which was a large accomplishment for me. It didn't matter to me how many life coaching clients I had, no matter how many suits or shoes I sold, no matter how many classes I taught, or groups I spoke to, or great ideas I had, or even successful things or positions I had acquired...I still felt like I was not good enough because of something I did not have. I told my "self" that the one thing that I did not have was the degree, but as I began to clean my room a bit more I discovered that the negative "self" talk came from the negative "self" talk that I experienced as a child. There was anger all around me during the time when most of the child's mental development happens, and boy did I soak it up.

The only good memory of my father was him dancing in the living room of our home to the sounds of Parliament

Funkadelic. It was the funniest thing I had ever seen. I was around four or five years old at the time, and my daddy jumping around our living room pretending to be George Clinton was the first time I can honestly say I saw my father not in an angry space. It was almost like the music made daddy happy. I believe that was the moment in which I told my "self" that music is what should keep me happy, because it made my daddy happy. And to this day, I use music to take me away from negative head spaces.

Although I have this positive memory of my father, I also have several negative memories of him. The one that stands out the most for me is the memory of him not being there. In spite of all of the anger that I saw come from him towards my mother, and my sisters, and then to my little brother that was a new born baby and had done nothing to him, I saw my daddy as the best thing in my world. In my eyes, my daddy could do no wrong. I still believe that I am a "Daddy's Girl," but as a little girl, I would constantly think of my daddy and wonder what I had done to make him so angry that he could just walk away from me.

I believe in those moments of growing up seeing those negative outburst against my mother taught me to keep emotions to my "self" because if you express your "self" openly, then there would be negative consequences. The elder generation would say that "little children should be seen and not heard." So, since I could not talk to anyone, I would have to settle for talking to my own "self". Unfortunately, the only positive reinforcement was that of the negative behaviors that I witnessed which led to negative "self" talk.

You may have learned negative "self" talk from a situation similar to mine, or from your own personal struggles. The point is that our negative "self" talk stems from something in our past that was buried under the pile of clutter that has built up over the years. Here is where we pull back the layers of clutter to get to that smelly, rotten mess that is continuously fuming in our room. We do not see the issue in plain sight, but we know it is there because of the stench that breeds "stinkin' thinkin'."

It was scary for me to go back to those moments, but the good thing about going back to the past is that once you go there...you don't have to stay. Going back will help you to move forward. I encourage you to do this exercise in an effort to help you clean your room. You can find ways to encourage your "self". One of my teachers would joke about talking to her "self". She would say, "some times it's the most intelligent conversation that I will have all day." Well, if that is the case, then make the most intelligent conversation that you will have all day a conversation that is positive, encouraging, as motivating as possible. You can do this because you are in control of the conversation. You choose the subject, and the responses. Remember that whatever the mind conceives it can also achieve. So dream big! Then, encourage your "self" with positive "self" talk.

By the way, I learned that I did not need the validation of a college degree or the validation of my earthly father in order to realize that I could do all things with the mind that I have been blessed with by my father in heaven.

When the time is right, I believe that the opportunity will again present itself, and I will earn that college degree. Since I know that life happens and that I must continue on, it is okay to put this goal on

114

hold because I have discovered that the goal may not be SMART at the moment. If you realize this about one of your own goals, then do not be discouraged. Continued forward movement guarantees future opportunities and advancement.

"If you don't like something…change it. If you can't change it…change your attitude."

-Dr. Maya Angelou

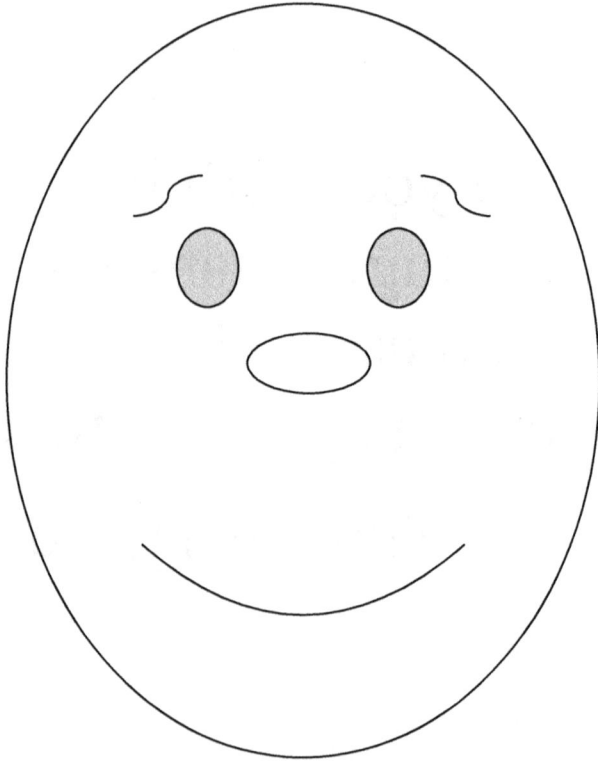

7

Attitude

The good, the bad, and the ugly

Surely it is easier to have a great attitude when things are going well. If the world was make of Cami Cakes, and I could eat them all day without gaining a pound, then of course keeping a positive attitude would be...a piece of cake. However, there are times when a bad attitude will jump out of nowhere, and ruin a perfectly good opportunity.

119

Some problems come just to see what you are made of. Remember God does not 'test' you, but your situation sure will. More often than not, maintaining the right attitude will result in a win-win for all involved. While you consider this next set of scenarios, be honest with what your first reaction would be if you were the subject. Write your answers below.

1. When you arrived to work, your boss escorts you into a conference room with the head of the human resources department to inform you that your position has been eliminated.

_____

_____

_____

_____

_____

_____

_____

2. You are a member of a team in which the team lead does not distribute the work equally to each team member.

_____

_____

_____

_____

_____

_____

_____

3. You confide in a friend some confidential information that they share with someone that you do not associate with, and the information comes back to you.

_____

_____

_____

_____

_____

_____

_____

4. Your husband confesses to being dishonest about his paycheck, and puts your finances in jeopardy.

_____

_____

_____

_____

_____

_____

_____

5. An amazing opportunity is presented, and your decision to take advantage of the opportunity brings out the worst in someone that you thought would celebrate with you.

_____

_____

_____

_____

_____

_____

_____

In each instance above, you could easily allow an emotional reaction instead of a conscience response. Pay close attention here. You could easily ALLOW...here is the word that puts you in control. However, if you are dealing with a "dirty room," then you could easily get distracted by something or some negative feeling buried amongst all of your junk. Any one of the scenarios above could awaken the stench of some dirty emotional junk buried in the corner of your room. This junk that has been lying around and waiting for just the right moment to release a venomous thought, that causes that emotional reaction. We act on that thought instead of thinking things through, and then next thing you know your attitude has turned negative, and your reaction is outside of your control. Can you say...MELTDOWN? The finger waving, neck rolling, foot stomping, teeth sucking, triple blinking attitude monster comes out and jumps all over the place then causes a scene beyond biblical proportions. This negative reaction will never help you nor will it create a positive outcome. You must stay in control of your emotions and consider your response instead of issuing a heated reaction.

The ability to control your response is within you. However, there are times when we surrender our control to the junk. Here is another reason why cleaning our room is important. Mental and emotional junk is just as bad, if not worse than physical junk.

At least with physical junk, you can actually see it with the naked eye. You can pick it up and put it in its place or you can throw it away. Emotional junk, on the other hand, is not so easy to deal with. You have to search for it and once you find it, then you have to confront or even re-live it in order to put it in its place or throw it away. Believe it or not, some bad experiences are actually lessons in disguise.

They could be lessons for you, or a lesson that you can teach someone else.

Just in case you were wondering, each of the scenarios in this chapter did indeed happen to me. I can truly say that in at least two of those situations, I did indeed allow my emotions to control my reaction. After some time, and a few wisdom growth spurts, I am able to see how I could have handled those situations a little differently. I was disappointed in the way that I reacted in some of those situations, but proud of the way that I handled others.

We have to consider the junk so that we can determine if it has a place in our room, or if it needs to be thrown away. For some, this will not be an easy task, but the sooner you do it the better. Consider the way that you chose to react to the earlier scenarios. First of all, did you react, or respond? Second, if you chose to react negatively, use the "Five Why" exercise that I talk about in the book "Seven Days to Satisfied" to try and determine what was really behind your reaction.

Third, try to think the scenario through in order to come up with a positive response instead. If you need help with this, then you may want to consider bringing on a life coach or therapist to work with. Someone who can be bias to your situation is a better choice than someone who could possibly judge you, or share your issues with the wrong person. OUCH!

In the beginning of this chapter I said that it is easy to have a great attitude when things are going well. However, I also believe that it is just as easy to have a good attitude when things are not going so well. I say this because when we choose to stay in control of what goes into and comes out of our room, then we set the standard for our own "self". When our room is clean, we are not overwhelmed by junk which clouds our vision and affects our attitude. Let's look at the definition.

ATTITUDE n. 1.) A complex mental state involving beliefs and feelings and values and dispositions to act in certain ways.

Now that you see the real definition of the word attitude, can you see how some junk in your room can alter yours? Go back to Dr. Angelou's quote at the beginning of this chapter and read it out loud. Then, take a deep breath, and read the quote out loud once more. Then, take another deep breath, and quiet your mind. Repeat the quote once more. Try to use this exercise to create a means to improve the attitude of your own "self". Try to find a way to see the positive in all situations. From this point forward, always try to respond, and never react.

This takes time, but I am sure you can do it. Commit to having a better, more positive attitude. Remember to always take the time to think it through. Take an extra 30 seconds to evaluate the situation in order to respond appropriately instead of emotionally reacting to a situation because that could make the situation worse.

Finding a way to clear your mind, or "release" as I would say will help you remain at peace even when your emotions attempt to get the best of you. Here is where an extracurricular activity, regular meditation, or even a life coach could come in handy. I try to take a walk, listen to music, find a quiet place to pray, or remove my "self" from the issue until I can get my emotions in check. What are some things that you can do to bring your "self" back to thinking rationally? List them below.

1. _____

2. _____

3. _____

You can have a long list of 10 things, or a short list of just three things. As long as you have an outlet of some sort in order to ensure that you are able to peacefully respond to your issue with a good attitude.

Go back to scenarios in the beginning of this chapter and answer them with a better attitude. What differences do you see? Think about some of your own scenarios, and consider how you could have handled things differently had you responded with a better attitude. What things could you do to change your attitude? Commit to doing those things for your own "self" today. Remember that your attitude determines your altitude.

"Courage is the most important of all the virtues because without courage, you can't practice another virtue consistently."

-Dr. Maya Angelou

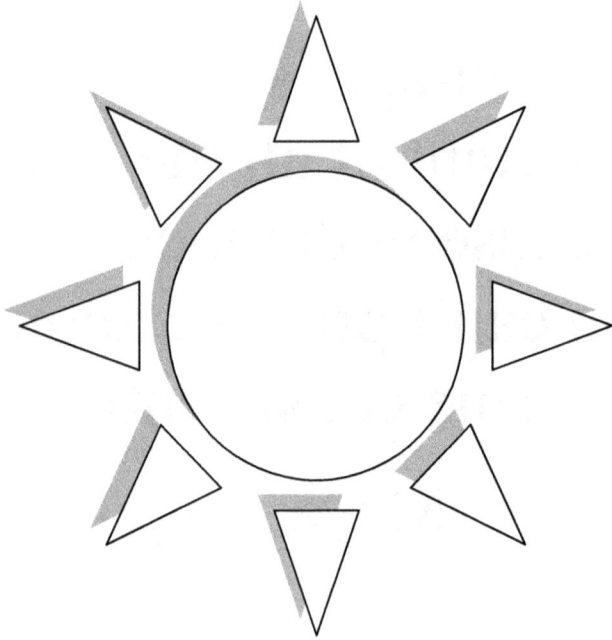

8

Confidence

The keys to the Kingdom

In my own opinion, courage and confidence go hand in hand. You really can't have one without the other.

Confidence is knowing that you can do it, courage is the push you give your "self" to do it. When we were born, we had no since of fear. We were confident little human beings that relied on our God given abilities and relied solely our instincts.

When we were strong enough to roll over...we simply rolled over. It did not matter if we were close to the edge of the bed. When we were strong enough to crawl we simply ascended to our hands and knees and crawled. We had no since of fear, but we had a built in, over abundance of confidence and courage fueled by our God given instincts. So what happened to that? Where did that fear come from? What took away our God given instinct to "Just Do It" as the folks at Nike command us to?

I can remember when I was around four years old. My mother would send me and my sisters to bed. I shared a room with my middle sister, while my older sister had a room of her own. Our room was situated so that our bunk beds looked out of the door of the bedroom, through the dining room and into the kitchen. From the top bunk where I slept, I had a clear view of the refrigerator. Now there really isn't anything scary about that right? Wrong!

My imagination certainly would get the best of me on many occasions as a child. I could never bring my "self" to jump out of my bed to go to the bathroom in the middle of the night. I could jump from the top bunk all day long if my mom would let me, but I could not do it a night with the lights off.

What was the difference? Well...when jumping down during the day,

I could see where I would land after taking the jump, but at night it seemed much farther down with the lights off as oppose to at night with the lights on. I was afraid to jump because I thought I would continue to fall. It felt like I was jumping into a dark hole with no bottom.

Sometimes I would think that maybe my daddy would catch me, but most times he was not there because he left after yet another argument with my mother (I believe he did that on purpose). I was terrified because my mind would see monsters that would freeze me in fear. I was unable to move because I would hear footsteps in my ears thinking that if I moved, then the monsters would get me. I was stuck.

I carried those "monsters" around in my room up into adulthood. I would still hear those footsteps every time I had to do something out of my comfort zone and just like when I was afraid to jump out of the safety of my bed, I was just as scared to jump outside of what I felt was safe to me mentally.

What I considered safe were those things that were normal. Working a 9-to-5 job was normal, sitting in the audience was normal, having no money was normal, being in debt was normal, manipulating love was normal, wanting more but not doing what it took to get it was normal...keeping a junky room was normal.

It took some time to figure out that my natural instinct to be confident was buried under the shadow of the refrigerator/monster that I could see from my childhood bedroom, hidden deep within the footsteps/my own heart beat that I thought was the monster coming to get me. I had developed a fear that kept me from moving beyond my normal. I had destroyed my own confidence.

Now of course with time comes wisdom. I can recognize the junk in my room and decipher why my confidence is sometimes stifled. If you are having some challenges confronting some of the junk in your room, then I highly recommend a life coach or counselor of some sort to help you get mentally organized. I know from experience that cleaning you room is not the easiest task. In fact, it can be downright overwhelming, but the process can bring you to the unveiling of a much stronger, more confident "self" that has the courage to go ahead and push your "self" past your normal.

Is there something that you have always wanted to do? Have you watched others become successful and wonder why you have not been so "fortunate"? Here is one that I have heard many times before...have you missed your calling? In the beginning of your life I believe there was an assignment place inside of you. There is indeed a plan for your life, and because of all of the junk in our room it can be hard to see it. Believe me, it is there. Sometimes we have to use the junk in our rooms to complete that assignment, so in this case the junk can be useful. Now I know that I have said since the beginning of this book that we need to clean our rooms, and we do indeed. However, for the sake of me not looking like a hypocrite, allow me to clarify.

As a real estate agent, I sometimes have to help my clients get organized in order to prepare their homes for sale. I recommend that they use plastic bins to separate those things that they will place, those things that they will pack, and those things they will pitch. Things that you would place are those things that you use regularly and will make the space visually appealing, so you would PLACE them appropriately. Things that you would pack are those things that you can still use, but make the room look cluttered so you PACK them away for later use. Things that you would pitch are those things that you have no use for and make your room congested so you PITCH, or throw them away.

Using the "Place, Pack, and Pitch" approach when cleaning your room will help you organize your thought processes just like it helps my real estate clients with the process of organizing their homes. For example, maybe an elder, a spiritual advisor, your mentor, or life coach said something that you consider a good word of advice. You know that you can and will use that word again in the near future, so you PLACE it on the forefront of your mind in order to retrieve it quickly if necessary. I try to keep encouraging words, scriptures, even song lyrics in this position.

Experiences, positive or negative, are those things that I PACK away. Now some people may disagree with me here on packing away negative experiences, but I believe that there are lessons in all experiences that we can glean from, and even help others with. Remember, after you "touch it once" that means you have addressed it, so referring to it again is okay especially if seeing that you were able to overcome it will bless someone else.

Last, those things that I PITCH are those things (and people) that are preventing me from moving to my next level. Constantly carrying needles things (and people) only keep you dragging junk from one corner of your room to the other instead of actually cleaning it.

If you ask your "friend" to come and help you move, and they bring your favorite snacks and begin talking you into keeping that stash of old plastic bags from all of your grocery store trips that you have been saving for years just in case you need them,

147

then this may be a "friend" that you need to call some other time.

Seriously speaking there are people that will show you that they will not encourage, or value your progress. You must be careful here because it is easy to become confused about this one. Some things (and people) that you may believe you are obligated to PLACE, should actually be PITCHed. Those 'people' and those 'things' you must learn to live, and love from a distance.

Once you get room organized, then you will see your "self" from a more clear perspective. You are able to make decisions that are not fueled only by emotions. You are able to respond, and not react to

148

situations positive or negative in a more productive fashion. Your level of confidence will increase simply because you are not concerned about the monsters coming to get you, and you will have the courage to jump into your destiny simply because you do not have to look through a junky room to find your courage and your confidence. Both your courage and confidence is in its proper PLACE for easy access.

"Look what you've already come through! Don't deny it. Say I'm stronger than I thought I was."

-Dr. Maya Angelou

9

Good, Clean Strength

You are in control

I know that this task will not be an easy one. Making the decision to clean your room takes a tremendous amount of strength, and commitment. You must be willing to make an investment in your own "self" in order to reap the vast benefits that come with a clean room. Many may say that you free up space for more junk, but if you make sure that you control what comes into your room, then all will be well.

I am the first to admit that I am a control freak. When it came to people that I care about, projects that I am in charge of, or businesses that I ran, I wanted to be in control of every aspect of it. Right up until I had a complete meltdown. Every bulb in my star had blown out. I lost money, business, time with my family, and ultimately…my "self." I learned the hard way that I was not in control, but I was in fact being controlled.

A junky room already has control of you, but if you are not careful the projects that you take on, business or personal, will take control of you too.

Once upon a time, I would tout on a regular basis that I was Superwoman. When someone asked me to take on another project I would brag about the "S" on my chest without once taking into consideration the junk in my room, or the effect that it had on any of my old or new projects. In my mind, I could do it all. I was a one-woman, well oiled machine.

When the conflict between my mentality and my reality came to a head, everything had spiraled out of control. My life was completely out of balance and it took a toll on me, my family, and my business. I had to come to grips with my weaknesses, and find some way to begin to strengthen my "self" immediately.

Now this did not happen overnight for me, so I do not expect for these changes to happen overnight for you. Once again, the journey of 1,000 miles starts with one step. Consider getting some help with this one. A life coach can help you with your plan, and help you set goals. A life coach can also become a sounding board for ideas, hold you accountable, and cheer you on to success.

When I meet my clients for the first time, I ask them, "What is it that you want to accomplish?" This question forces a decision, and that is the first step. MAKE A DECISION! It is important that you do not become overwhelmed and become paralyzed by over analyzing the problem.

That good ole 'analysis paralyses' and 'incline blind' will keep you from moving forward every time.

So, what do you want to accomplish? Do you have a project, or several projects that you want to complete this month…this year? What is your plan? Have you written down your goals? What kind of help do you need? What resources will you utilize? How much can you delegate to trusted members of your team? Yes you read that right. If you are a control freak like me, then you too will have to learn that it takes team work to make the dream work.

I could not do it all alone and you may have to come to grips with the fact that you may need to let some pieces of your project go. Truth is, if you allow yourself to delegate, then you can also give someone else an opportunity to shine along with you. In getting help, you will help someone else. That is an accomplishment within itself.

Business projects are important, but there will be no successful business projects without successful personal projects. This brings me back to your room. We have to make sure that we have a plan, goals, and help with cleaning our room. More importantly, we need to make sure that we allow enough time (the T in our SMART goal acronym) to accomplish those task that we established. No one knows you better than you, and sometimes we have to take a step back and look at our own "self" in order to ensure that the past that created us does not continue to delay us.

I encourage you to make and keep this commitment, and invest in your own "self." Believe me you are worth it…YOU ARE WORTH IT! Now, clean your room.

Notes:_____

_____

_____

_____

_____

_____

_____

_____

_____

_____

_____

_____

_____

_____

_____

_____

_____

_____

_____

_____

_____

_____

_____

_____

_____

_____

_____

_____

_____

_____

_____

_____

_____

_____

_____

_____

_____

_____

_____

_____

_____

_____

_____

_____

_____

_____

_____

_____

_____

_____

_____

_____

_____

_____

_____

_____

_____

_____

_____

_____

_____

_____

I was watching an episode of News One Now with Roland Martin on the morning of May 28, 2014. Looking forward to the comedians segment called Wildin' Out Wednesdays. Early in the program Roland was interrupted with the news of the passing of Dr. Maya Angelou. As he made the announcement from what he believed was a trusted source, I was shocked into silence. As he then repeated the news I felt a tear begin to roll down my face. I have never had the pleasure of meeting and sharing her presence in person, but I will always remember how much I admired her, and her body of work. I would refer to her as Mama Maya (as if she gave me permission to call her that) respectfully as I did most of my female elders, and hearing of her passing had me feeling like I had really lost one of my mothers. Watching her on screen, reading her work, listening to her voice, and partaking of her wisdom made her a silent part of the family.

I started this book months ago with quotes from other well-known names. However, when my "long distance" mentor went home to be with God I thought this would be a way to honor the way she inspired me to this little bit of greatness. With love and admiration I dedicate this book to the number one phenomenal woman...

Dr. Maya Angelou

"Trust in The Lord with all thy heart, and lean not unto thy own understanding. In all thy ways acknowledge him, and he will direct your paths"

-Proverbs 3:5-6

F. Dennelle Hickson

Author, Speaker, Life Coach

For coaching appointments, speaking
events, or personal appearances contact
us at:

(904) 428-8879

www.makeyournextmove.net

Coming soon!

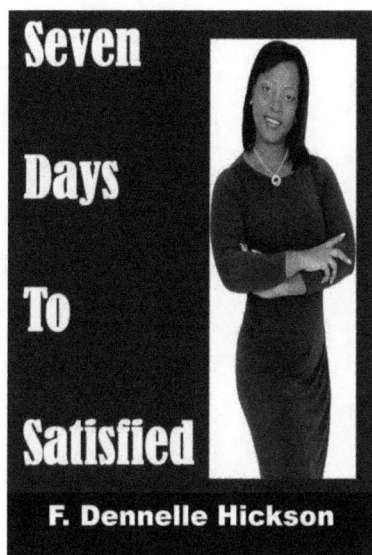

Seven Days To Satisfied

F. Dennelle Hickson

It doesn't take forever to go from bitter to better. "Seven Days to Satisfied" is the seven day breakdown journal that will help to produce a better you.

Visit us at:

www.MakeYourNextMove.net

www.ingramcontent.com/pod-product-compliance
Lightning Source LLC
LaVergne TN
LVHW091257080426
835510LV00007B/300